NOT MANIFESTING? THIS BOOK IS FOR YOU!

KATHLEEN MACKENZIE

Outskirts Press, Inc.
Denver, Colorado

Not Manifesting? This Book Is For You!

Outskirts Press, Inc.
http://www.outskirtspress.com

ISBN: 978-1-4327-1302-7

Outskirts Press and the "OP" logo are trademarks belonging to Outskirts Press, Inc.

PRINTED IN THE UNITED STATES OF AMERICA

AUTHOR'S NOTE

The intended reader for this little book is the person who genuinely aspires to be the best person possible. If you are someone who wants to venture outside of day-to-day existence, and manifest all good things, and want only good for everyone you encounter—then this book is for you. If you believe genuine love is your highest calling and you are up for a spiritual adventure—then this book is for you.

This book is meant for people already familiar with the Law of Attraction, Law of Deliberate Creation, Law of Allowing, etc. This is not a book for beginners; it is for people who clearly understand the concepts of deliberate creation but who are not seeing the desired results.

As you already understand, the Law of Attraction works, whether we are loving individuals or selfish and unloving. My interest in writing this little book is to help support the success of those people who want to make the world a better place for themselves and for all of us.

I emphasize that this book is written from my

personal experience and research. I have been researching and experiencing various aspects of spirituality for the past thirty-five years. I am sharing what works for me, and I believe with all my heart it will work for you as well. However, do I know with absolute certainty that life between lives, past-life regression, reincarnation, spirit guides, the life I have seen in another dimension, etc., are the absolute truth? The answer is that I cannot prove anything I am about to share with you in this book. I certainly do not rule out the possibility that someone could have a completely different experience and that experience could be true and accurate as well. What I share with you is what works for me and what has helped other people I know.

TRIAL AND ERROR

I have read countless books from many different authors about deliberate creation and attracting abundance. Every book I read and every lecture I attended said I could be, do, or have anything. I found myself spending lots of money, but with little result. Then, with trial and error, I did find what works for me and I am now deliberately creating. This book is written to share the information I have found that can help you to manifest your heart's desires as well.

You will read again about the Law of Attraction. However, it will contain new information for you. Most important, whatever your current situation, you can change it if you put this information into practice.

TABLE OF CONTENTS

CHAPTER 1
PROBLEMS MANIFESTING?

I f you are reading this book, then it's likely you are not manifesting your heart's desires with the degree of success you would like. In fact, you may believe you have not been able to manifest at all. You might be somewhere in between.

As I'm sure you know, there are many books, videos, conferences, cruises, and presentations on the subject of deliberate creation or the Law of Attraction. The presentations I have attended have been standing room only. I would always leave the presentation, or finish one of the books, and feel great. But after a short time, I was frustrated with the process once again. I knew I had to be missing something in the process, or I was missing a piece of the puzzle, because I was not manifesting what I thought I was focused on.

I have found what I believe to be the missing information, because my life is now working for me instead of against me. And I need to tell you right now—there is work involved. It is not simply focusing on what you desire with detachment, or any of the many attraction-based related themes. What happened to me is that I recognized I was reading the same information over again and over again. That information came from a variety of authors and channeled spirits such as Abraham in addition to the movie *The Secret*.

I realized that this information is not really new at all. If you are familiar with the Christian Bible, you will see its themes appear in the New Testament. I am not familiar with other religions' holy books, but I believe you would find related themes in them as well.

So if you have read books about deliberate creation, the Law of Attraction, manifesting abundance, etc., and if you are not feeling successful in your attempts to manifest your desires—know that you are not alone.

I hope this book will help you deliberately create the life you were born to live. If you follow the instructions found in these pages, you will begin to manifest your best and highest good.

CHAPTER 2
THE UNIVERSE? MY HIGHEST SELF? WHAT ARE THEY?

Different authors and lecturers have spoken of the higher self, the soul, the authentic self, map of reality, spirit guides, ego vs. spirit, and on and on. I decided I needed to settle this confusion for myself before I could move forward.

I used my experience of the Edgar Cayce-sponsored past-life regression programs I had attended and the research I had conducted over the past thirty-five years.

For readers who have never had a past-life regression, I want you to know that it is fascinating and very rewarding. The past-life regressionists I have used are licensed hypnotherapists who are graduates of the Edgar Cayce Foundation (the A.R.E.), located in Virginia Beach, Virginia.

You may not have been hypnotized, at least not by a certified or licensed hypnotist or hypnotherapist. But please know that it is not about stage enter-

3

tainment or about forcing someone to act or speak against his or her will.

Hypnosis brings someone to a stage where the brain is cycling more slowly, so the conscious self can access information that is normally hidden from it. Your level of awareness is such that you may not think you are being hypnotized at all! It is best to write down questions you'd like your regressionist to ask while you are in this state.

Based on my experience, I recommend that you use a hypnotist or hypnotherapist who is connected with the A.R.E., because these people are skilled in past-life readings. When you contact a hypnotherapist, at the very least ask if that person even believes in reincarnation.

Whether you are in the Washington, DC area or not, I recommend that you visit the website http://www.healthychoiceshome.com. Bob Minaert has studied past-life and between-lives regression hypnotherapy at the A.R.E., and is certified by the National Association of Transpersonal Hypnotherapists. He can help you visit past lives, your life in between lives, and he can help you get rid of any beliefs you have that no longer serve you. If you do not live in his area, he may be able to assist you by phone or help you to find someone where you reside.

Over the years, I had visited past lives but my interest at this point was in life between lives. I wanted to visit the place I inhabited between lives, the place where my next incarnation was planned. I wanted to see who was there and what this place looked like. I was looking for answers, but not necessarily adventure. Did I ever get a surprise!

During my first visit to life between lives, I saw what I would describe as my circle of family. They were dressed in purple- and yellow-trimmed robes, and they were quite tall. I recognized my mother, my aunt, and other relatives, neighbors, and friends. However, I did not see any animals. I have always loved animals and have had a few dogs I considered to be family. I loved them very much and it was heartbreaking when they died. Thankfully, that was one of the questions I had written for my hypnotherapist to ask. When I was asked if I saw Blackie or Joseph (my two Border Collies)...well, suddenly, I saw them. They came running into the area I was visiting. Blackie was my first babysitter when I was a child. He died more than 40 years ago. Joseph had died twelve years ago. They were so real that I burst into tears of happiness. Knowing that our pets accompany us caused me a profound sense of peace. However, that was not the central reason for my visit.

I first noticed that the members of my circle of family were standing and sitting in what I would describe as a modern town square. They were involved in deep conversation and did not seem to notice me at all. I stood there and watched for what seemed to be hours. I readily recognized the essence of each person. For example, my mother did not physically look like my mother. But, she was, without a doubt, the essence of my mother. I felt her love and kindness. I also recognized her perfect health. Mom died from Creutzfeldt-Jacob Disease (the human form of Mad Cow disease) and let me tell you, I've never seem such a horrific disease. But when I saw her, in that circle, her perfect health and loving peace was her true self.

The next surprise was when I noticed that this circle of family included people who were still alive on earth. However, these spirits appeared to be less dense. I then realized that part of me still exists on this plane, while part of me exists in physical form on earth. I truly understood that my higher self really *is* my higher self; that I am a multi-dimensional spirit living in a borrowed body. I knew then that my family circle and I had created a plan for me before I entered this physical lifetime, and that part of me stayed on the non-physical side of life while part of me adventured here. My non-physical self on the other side is my guide and has access to all the power and knowledge of the universe every minute of every day. I knew that communicating with my higher self and my circle of family could help me be, do, or have anything in this lifetime.

To say I was intrigued would be an understatement. I was definitely going back for more! What I have since learned keeps evolving and I will share what I am learning at a future time.

What I know now is that my life here on this planet was planned—by me—in the other dimension. I decided who my parents would be, where I would live, and what my life's purpose would be. People who have touched my life in profound ways have traveled here with me and are working out their life purposes as well. My higher self helps guide me because my higher self completely understands my life purpose. My free will allows me the daily choices that either move me closer to my purpose or further from my purpose. I realized that my free-will is a two-edged sword. I use it to move toward *and* to move away from my life purpose. I also realized that I purposely chose to live with limitations in this dimension, which explains many things. After a longtime of searching, I have found my connection to my higher self and have been able to align myself with my life purpose and with my higher self.

CHAPTER 3
TAKE COMPLETE
RESPONSIBILITY

First: take complete responsibility for your life as it is right now. I am speaking about everything: your relationships, your level of financial security, and the degree of your happiness.

Some authors claim that if anyone who has been harmed in an accident, had a stillborn baby, lost a son or daughter to war, or addicted to substances, that that person is completely responsible and have attracted all of that into their lives. I don't buy this. I believe that everyone comes to this dimension with a life purpose and with free will. We are free to make choices, both healthy and unhealthy. Others make choices for us (like being drafted to fight in the Vietnam war, for example). Perhaps we may decide, on the other side, to experience life here blind or to be born with health issues. We may have decided while on the other side to have different experiences and to use the contrast to more sharpen our experience. We did elect to come here with limitations. However, I am not going to say that each and every event in everyone's life has happened due to a life purpose. I believe we can waste our lives by delving into substance abuse and not taking any of the offers of help along the way to conquer this issue. We can waste our lives by turning to crime or by exerting such a degree of control over others that we actually destroy another human being. I do not believe anyone purposely attracts acts of domestic violence because it was a life purpose to suffer at the hands of a violent partner. We all make choices every day and these choices can bring us nearer to our life purpose or drive us further away. People who believe that this is the only life they will live—who believe that there is no soul or spirit inside their body—will have little compunction about inflicting harm on others because they believe there is no judgment. I realize that all I have said in this paragraph has little to nothing to do with the intention of this book. I just wanted to make myself clear on this issue because my intention is not to offend anyone who has suffered or is suffering.

So, again, accept complete responsibility for your life as it is right now, concerning your relationships, your level of financial security, and the degree of your happiness. Much if not all of the negative stuff we attract into our lives is due to fear- or anger-based attraction. It's the negative energy charge we give to our thoughts and to our feelings. If for some reason you believe you will always have hard luck or that you will always be poor or that you will never meet the right person in your life—then you are right. You will receive what you believe. If this is true, then you have to change your beliefs right now. You have to eliminate the beliefs that do not serve you and adopt beliefs that do serve you.

Every morning and every evening, as well as any time you have the opportunity (using the bathroom at work, etc.), look in the mirror and tell yourself that you love yourself. Look deeply into your eyes—the eyes are the gateway to the soul—and tell yourself that you love yourself. You cannot give to others what you do not have yourself. You cannot bring love to the world if you do not love yourself. So, no matter what kind of shape you are in right now, forgive yourself for your failings, look into your own eyes, and tell yourself that you love yourself unconditionally and that you fully accept the person you are. If you do this for a minimum of one month, you will notice a big difference in your daily life. People will begin smiling in your direction more often. They will sense an attractive peace about you because your authentic self will be operating more and more each and every day.

If you are currently feeling financial stress, accept the fact that you have attracted this situation into your life through thoughts that did not serve you. Perhaps your parents were poor and, by their behavior and words, taught you to believe that money is scarce. You need to forgive them, bless them, and move on with your life. You must replace your limiting belief of financial scarcity with one of the abundance of the universe. The reason affirmations do not work is because most people say them without emotion, or else the affirmations are just not believable to your ego. Used correctly, affirmations can override your current limiting belief. Do not use an affirmation that states you are wealthy and flowing with abundance right now. You know it's not true, so that affirmation will never fool the subconscious into believing it. However, there is a right and powerful way to override your current limiting belief; used correctly, affirmations can do it for you.

CHAPTER 4
BE GENUINE

The first self-examination you must do is to determine if you are actually genuine. Why is this important? Because of the Law of Attraction. You know what it says: you get back from the universe what you put out into it. It's a variant of the old saying, "Garbage in, garbage out." And it works the other way, too, of course: put out good things and you'll get good things back. So you attract what you are—what you really are, at your core.

Most of us have spent many years thinking negative thoughts and doing negative things, even if we fool ourselves that we're not. We do it in our homes, at work, in the grocery store, on the road, while falling asleep. If there is any truth to "you reap what you sow," then it stands to reason that a mind filled with negative thoughts will attract negative energy and negative results. This is why you have to be genuine.

Believe it or not, the first step to being genuine—going back to what I said in the last chapter—

is this: you must love yourself unconditionally, right now, no matter where you are or what you are doing. You may be reading this book from your home or from a prison cell. It doesn't matter. No matter where you are, accept yourself unconditionally. You start being genuine by accepting yourself and being genuine with yourself. Then you can be genuine with others.

In order to be genuine, what you say and what you do must be the same. You may say you believe in accepting other people at whatever point they are in their personal growth and that you love others and want their best and highest good. But if you are impatient with co-workers, friends, or strangers who drive slowly in the left lane or who do not live up to some of your standards, then you are not genuine.

You have to look at the places in your life where you are not the person you claim to be, the person you desire to be. Do you love someone but often criticize that person? Do you love your spouse, your partner, your significant other—but find fault in the way he or she cleans the house, cooks dinner, makes love, fixes the washing machine, mows the lawn, etc., etc.? Do you claim to be enlightened but withhold forgiveness? Do you listen to gossip? Do you take part in the undoing of others? Do you spread gossip? Do you withhold comment when others are gossiping? If any of this applies to you, the duplicity has to stop. You must bring your best self forward and live through your higher self. Every time you hear yourself beginning to engage in conversation where someone is harmed—where that person is marginalized or diminished by your words or by your entertaining someone else's words—you must stop immediately. Your life cannot be about harming anyone else. You must actively love the other, recognizing that everyone has something to give to you and that you have something to give to everyone. If you cannot think of a positive word to say about someone else, then say nothing at all. If you are engaged in conversation that turns to criticism about someone, you must disengage, even if the person you are talking with is your boss, your life partner, your best friend, or anyone else in your life. It is really not OK to harm anyone.

This is why we must not judge anyone. We do have the tendency to think in negative terms. We judge others without any invitation to do so. Who are we to set the standards for the world around us? We easily take on the role of setting the standards for everyone. How often have you passed judgment on strangers? We judge them for the way they wear their hair, select their clothes, are too skinny or too fat, speak with an accent, and on and on. Do you pass judgment on others because of their nationality or even what part of the country they come from? How often do you read or tell dirty jokes? Do you really think Yankees are cold and uncaring? Do you really think people from our most southern states speak in a foreign language? Or, do you think people from our most northern states speak in a foreign language? Do you believe all our elected officials are crooked? Do you believe you belong to the only real religion, the only one that will bring you to heaven? Does your religion have a lock on God and salvation?

As you can easily see, passing judgment or diminishing others is very easy for us to do. We do it every day.

Love is a decision. Once you make the decision to bring love to the world, you will be on your way to a new and wonderful life. The decision to be genuine removes blocks to manifesting your desires. Love is a decision based not on feelings but on choice.

At this point, I'd like you to stop reading and just give this chapter some thought. I'd like you to consider how you live your life and if are you proud of the person you have become. Do you live in your head or do you live in your heart? Living in your head is fine if you like living there. Living in your heart and consulting your head will be the beginning of miracles.

When Alice fell down the rabbit hole, she found a very new and different world. It was fascinating, it was scary, and it was a trip Alice would never forget. When we came to this life, we accepted that we jumped down that rabbit hole and that we would find our way out of our rabbit hole. We arrived with the ability to create anything we want with our thoughts and feelings. However, since we did not retain our in-between life memories, we have to find our way back to our life's purpose. You have reached the point in your life when you began to question your life's purpose.

The purpose of this book is to help you find your way back to your life's purpose and to create the life you want.

CHAPTER 5
KEEP YOUR WORD

The Law of Attraction is working all the time and we are creating all the time. What is in your life right now is the result of your own creation. I know you may resist that statement if your life seems filled with things you would never create for yourself ... but it's true. What you are experiencing now is what you have invited into your life through the law of attraction.

Step back and take a look at yourself. Do you keep your word? At first blush, you are probably saying that of course you are good for your word. BUT do you break your promises to yourself? Have you ever promised to exercise every day, or made a New Year's resolution to lose weight? Have you promised yourself that you would be patient with your significant other? How many promises that you made to yourself have you broken? Or turn it around: how many promises have you made to yourself that you have kept?

If you had a friend who constantly broke promises to you, just maybe you would re-evaluate your friendship. Who wants to be friends with a liar? How valuable is the friend you cannot believe or cannot count on to follow through with their promises? But here we are, lying to ourselves on a regular basis.

The universe cannot accept all our mixed messages and deliver our manifestation intentions. Any kind of mixed message is powerless. Mixed messages have to stop immediately.

You begin with yourself. When you make a promise or commitment to yourself or to others, you must keep your word. You must give your word power and strength. The universe must recognize that you are genuine and consistent. Beginning right now, take your promises and commitments seriously. If you make a promise or commitment to yourself or to anyone else, *keep your word*. If you know you will not follow through on a promise or commitment, *do not* make that promise or commitment. Reach down into your gut and find the fortitude to promise or commit for only those things that you will follow through on.

Eliminate the word *try*. When someone says, "I'll try to make it there," they are giving themselves room to not follow through. When someone tells me they will try to do something, I now take it as almost a guarantee they will not do it. For me, the word *try* is just a polite way of saying, "Don't count on me." So eliminate it from your vocabulary. You will either commit or not. You will either do or not do. Make your word powerful. When your word becomes powerful, so do your intentions and the creative energy within you.

CHAPTER 6
GENEROSITY

Generosity is not only about giving away money or loaning money to others at a low interest. We need to shift our thinking from equating generosity with money and think instead of spiritual generosity.

Do you know the names of the people who, on a regular basis, serve you? You may think that no one serves you and that you don't employ housekeepers or gardeners. But do you know the name of the person who cleans your office? Do you know the name of the person who empties the trash from your cubicle at night? Do you know the name of your mail carrier? How about the lady at the laundromat who washes or folds your clothes—or the one who cleans the machines and floors of that laundromat so you are more comfortable? Perhaps she is also the person who changes the rolls of toilet paper in the rest room. How do you treat the person who waits on you in a restaurant or cleans your hotel room?

Have you ever shopped at a member warehouse? If you have, you must have noticed the free samples available to you as you shop. Manning the free samples are employees of that warehouse. Do you know they have to stand at their station all day (minus lunch and breaks) and that they have a quota to sell of that particular item on that particular day? They are not punished for not making the quota, but it does come in handy for them when they are up for a raise. How do you treat these people? When they ask if you'd like a sample, do you politely decline instead of just ignoring them?

So many of us expect others to wait on us because "it's their job" and they are getting paid to do that job. That is true. However, you are a spirit living in an acquired body and you know now that you have a purpose in this dimension. One purpose on this side of life is to love others as you would have them love you. The people who serve you deserve your love and respect. You need to start recognizing others around you right now. How do you do this? To address by name the person who empties your office trash, who picks up trash from the front of your driveway or takes it at the recycling center is an act of love. Don't know his or her name? Ask!

If you have enough money to go to a restaurant for lunch or dinner, consider that someone has prepared your table before you even sit down and that someone waits on your table. The service usually includes taking your order to your exact specifications and delivering each appetizer, entrée, dessert, drinks, and coffee, while refilling your water and checking on your dining satisfaction throughout your meal. And finally, it includes someone cleaning up after you are finished. In response to your service, please, in addition to leaving a generous tip (20% of the bill or more), say something to your server about his or her service and express your appreciation.

Perhaps you have never seen the invisible person who empties your cubicle trash at night. In that case, leave a note once in a while thanking the person for a job well done. Leave a holiday card for that person during the holiday season. Let this invisible person know you appreciate the service provided.

We have no idea what the impact is on someone when we take the time to smile and say hello, or when we take the time to learn the name of the person who usually bags our groceries. When we learn the names of those people who serve us or who live on the periphery of our lives—and when we use their names with a simple smile and a thank you—we will be practicing generosity of the spirit. We will be actively loving others and we will see miracles finding their way to us. Whatever we give out, we get back tenfold.

If you give of yourself generously to others, the universe will give back to you. Whatever you give, the universe will return, multiplied. And, due to the law of attraction, you will get back what you give multiplied – whether what you give out is negative or positive. So begin to intentionally treat others with love, respect, and forgiveness.

CHAPTER 7
YOU ARE WHAT YOU BELIEVE

You've heard the saying that you are what you eat. We all know that the saying is true. What is also true is that you are what you believe. Let's see why this is important to deliberate creation. What you believe is more important than what you think is true. What you believe is in your heart. What you think is true resides in your head. You may think it is true to bless those who curse you or to forgive anyone who has caused you harm—but when you are getting the worst of things in a bad situation, what you believe will emerge.

Why do you believe what you believe? You were not born with your beliefs. You came into your beliefs through your experiences in life. I was taught that my religion was the one true religion and that only those who adhered to it were going to heaven. Everyone else, those who were living in incorrect religions, could come on over and join my religion (so they could go to heaven as well). As a child, I came to understand that the best time to die was to drop dead immediately after swallowing the host at communion. If I dropped dead then, I would not have the opportunity to have any bad thoughts or do any bad deeds (like disobeying my parents). I went to the nine First Fridays services to get something called a plenary indulgence, so that all the bad stuff I must have done in the past would be completely forgiven and I could bypass Purgatory and go straight to see Saint Peter at the gates of heaven if I died soon thereafter. I believed all the priests in my church were directly descended from the Apostle Peter. I believed that I could not enter another church unless it was my denomination; in an emergency, I could enter an Episcopal church.

I share this single set of beliefs (of many) to illustrate the fact that if what I believed was really truth, then everyone would believe the same thing. There is only one version of truth. I do not believe today that one individual religion capitalizes on truth and has the one and only God, and that everyone else has to find their way to that religion or God will surely punish them.

If I still believed those things today, I would be locked in a reactive life, working very hard, and having very little in terms of true happiness and the freedom to deliberately create.

If someone asks you what you believe and you say you believe you are a compassionate person but then you curse the person who cuts you off in traffic—do you really believe it? When something happens to us that upsets our beliefs, it is an opportunity to see what we are really made of and what we really believe. If you open a can of orange juice, orange juice will pour out. What comes out of you when you are shaken?

As an example, for years I believed in love and forgiveness, that we should bless those who curse us, and do unto others as we would like them to do unto us. Out of the blue, my position at work was eliminated and I was to be unemployed within the next two weeks. I also found out that a person in my department had spread rumors about me for almost ten years, saying I was difficult to work with and that I was, pretty much, a terrible person. There was a new boss in the agency with new folks in leadership. This person was able to influence the new boss in the agency to eliminate my position, leaving me unemployed with nothing to catch my fall.

What do you think happened? Did I forgive, bless, and embrace the folks who were responsible for this situation? No! I was angry. I was really, really angry and I wanted to destroy these folks. (At the time, I did not know who these folks were or why this had happened.) But this illustrates that when my beliefs (my can of orange juice) were shaken, what poured out of me was anger, fear, resentment, and the like. It also illustrates that when the chips were down, I did not accept that I had attracted this into my life. I blamed others!

To make a long story short, I recognized my true self, forgave my enemies, was thankful for my situation, and decided to learn what I needed to do to move forward. On the last day of my employment, a position in the agency was offered to me. I had not applied for it and I didn't even know it existed. I was able to accept that position, continue to be employed, continue to have health insurance, and continue my path of learning the art and meaning of deliberate creation. This incident was probably one of my best experiences. There is much more to this story and someday I will share it. However, this little book is not about me and my story, it's about helping you to begin to live an effortless, abundant life.

Take time to examine your genuine beliefs. Then determine whether your beliefs are working for you and supporting your success, or are they no longer serving you? If your beliefs are no longer serving you, then you must have the courage to step out of your current beliefs and adopt beliefs that will serve you. The belief that you have the power to create your life on purpose and that you have the capacity to bring love and light into this life is a powerful belief that will be the cause of miracles. This book begs you to take the risk of leaving self- or other-imposed beliefs that no longer serve you and embark on a new journey: of being an enlightened soul living in an acquired body creating your life on purpose.

CHAPTER 8
JESUS

You may or may not believe that Jesus is the Son of God, who died on the cross for our sins and rose from the dead to show us the way. You may be a born-again Christian or you may be unsure of what you think of him. But if you are reading this book, you are probably open to agreeing that Jesus of Nazareth was, at the very least, an incredible teacher.

Jesus has retained world-wide influence centuries after his death. He is quoted all over the world in church services, books, daily conversations, etc. For Christians, he is risen from the dead and is the Son of God. After thousands of years, he is still not thought of as a fraud. He is still believed to be the Son of God by millions of people all over the earth. At the very least, he is thought of as a great teacher. Given those credentials, I'd like to spend a little time with one teaching of Jesus. This teaching will move you closer to manifesting your heart's desire and living the life you were meant to live.

In the eighth chapter of the Gospel of John, Jesus teaches us about judging others. This lesson hit me deeply when I was much younger, but I have found it is a most difficult lesson to learn and live. I am not going to quote it verbatim from the Bible (I happen to be using the King James Version, but any version will be fine). I would be surprised if you are not already familiar with this teaching.

Jesus was at the Mount of Olives one night and early in the morning he went into the temple to teach the people. This was an opportunity for the scribes and Pharisees to bring to him a woman who was caught in the act of adultery. They wanted Jesus to agree that she should be stoned to death, in accord with the Law of Moses. They were putting Jesus on the spot. They continued to ask until Jesus finally answered. Jesus answered by saying, "He that is without sin among you, let him first cast a stone at her." Well, each person there stood, struck by their own conscience, because they knew, regardless of how holy they appeared, that they had sinned. They quietly left, one by one, until Jesus and the woman were left alone. Jesus then pointed out that the accusers had left and that no one was there any longer who wanted her to be stoned to death. Jesus also told her that he did not condemn her and to go now and "sin no more." We don't know what happened to the woman after that. She may have continued to be in an adulterous relationship or she may not. The point of the story is: who are we to judge anyone else, if our own hands are not clean?

NOT MANIFESTING?

One of elements of being genuine is to not hold yourself up as a judge over anyone else in your daily life. I am not talking about our judges, police, or probation officers, whose daily work is to come to judgment about others. They must judge. I hope, if you are a judge, probation, or police officer, you are judging from the heart and trying to protect the community as well as help the respondent when the help is appropriate and available.

Most of us are not in positions of legally judging others. So for most of us, the lesson is simple to learn and difficult to live. Simply put: do not judge others. Even if you have had a similar experience, you are not that person and you do not know how the other person feels. If you hear a rumor, you do not know if it is true. If you repeat the rumor, you continue to hurt that person at an even deeper level. Even if some nasty story someone has shared with you turns out to be the truth (say, for example, that someone actually did get caught being inappropriate with the boss), it's not helping you or the world to be repeating it or to be laughing about it.

Blowing out someone else's candle does not make ours burn more brightly.

CHAPTER 9
THE OVERLOOKED POWER OF FORGIVENESS

We are all made up of energy and our energy vibrates on different levels. If we are afraid or angry, our energy is reduced to a very low vibration. But if we are joyful and have an attitude that embraces gratitude and love, our energy accelerated to a very high vibration. Sounds easy, and it is easy—if your energy is clear and moving freely. You have heard of your energy centers, called chakras. If an energy center is blocked, your energy is not moving freely. You may also, without even knowing it, be stuck in limiting beliefs, or you may be holding onto unforgiveness.

I was taught by my mother that withholding forgiveness hurts me more than it hurts the person I refuse to forgive. Embarrassing as it is to tell you, it took me forty years to understand what my mother was teaching me. However, I can tell you right now that withholding forgiveness is a huge block to manifesting your heart's desires. I will share two instances of my unforgiveness to illustrate what I'm saying here.

During an energy clearing session, I realized I had unforgiveness toward my mother for making me take piano lessons as a child. It was intense for me at the time, but laughable now. We had a piano and we were relatively poor. So my mother had my brother and me take piano lessons. He loved it and he played beautifully. His fingers danced over the keys as he played song after song to entertain my mother and grandmother. He played *Danny Boy* for my grandmother and *Tennessee Waltz* for my mother. At Christmas, it was *Silent Night*, *Joy to the World*, and all the wonderful Christmas songs. He would play, my mother would sing along, and the Christmas tree would sparkle and shine. His piano playing produced magic in our house and gave my mother hours and hours of happiness. Then there was me. I would miss the keys, and mess up the G or F clef. I had no understanding of beat or rhythm, and I hated the piano more and more as each grueling day passed. I had to take piano lessons once a week during lunch—a good lunch spoiled every single week. My piano teacher also taught my brother. She reminded me each week that my brother was such a gifted player and wondered out loud if my brother and I were even related! Finally, the time arrived when my piano teacher told my mother that she was wasting her money sending me to piano lessons. To my relief, the dreaded piano lessons abruptly halted and I was free once again. But I wasn't, really. I also felt angry for being forced to take piano lessons and being humiliated by living in the shadow of my brother's talent (this also applied to grammar school, but that's another story), and I felt guilty for not mastering playing the piano. I let my mother down. When these memories floated to my consciousness during the session, it was easy to forgive my mother, my brother, and myself. I could feel my spirit become lighter when I forgave from my heart with a high vibrational match.

I came home from the energy clearing experience knowing how unforgiveness creates huge blocks and barriers to energy movement. I asked my Higher Self to show me areas of unforgiveness that remained. I thought that I would have an easy time knocking off one unforgiveness after another, because forgiving my mother and brother for the piano experience was so easy. Now on to my second example.

I realized I was holding unforgiveness toward a deceased aunt. My aunt Gin had died when I was sixteen years old. My feelings toward her became the closest I had ever come to hatred. I resented breathing the same air and sharing the same planet with her. When she died, my mother was thankful that I attended her wake and funeral service. On our way to the service (a few hours' drive in a neighboring state), my mother told me how good it was that I was going. My response? I told my mother I was just making sure she was dead.

To make a very long story short, my family lived in the childhood home of my dad, and his mother lived with us. My parents had purchased the home

from them years before I was born. My father died
when I was twelve years old, the day after Christmas;
my grandmother died the following August, when she
was 89. That left my mother and me in the house, because my brother was in college. I will not mention
the hurtful things I saw my aunt do when her mother,
my grandmother, was dying. After my grandmother
was buried, I thought that was the last I'd see of Aunt
Gin. However, one day a few weeks after the burial,
my mother and I were sitting in the living room talking when the phone rang and it was Aunt Gin! I heard
my mother's end of the conversation and by looking
at her, I knew something was brewing! She told Gin
that she owned the house and never to set foot in it
again. When she got off the phone, she told me that
Aunt Gin had called to inform my mother that she
(and I) had thirty days to vacate the house because
Aunt Gin was turning it into a duplex and would be
using it as income property. Aunt Gin was the oldest
of the living children of my grandmother, who died
without a will, so she assumed that she now owned
the house (it was her childhood home as well). Even
though nothing could come of my aunt's greedy intention, I felt hatred for her. The saying the "enemy of
my friend is my enemy" could be translated for me as
the "enemy of my mother is my enemy." This was the
straw that broke the camel's back. I didn't have much
to say that day because my words would have alarmed
my mother. There are more examples of Aunt Gin's
unkindness, but there is no need to share them.
When it came to forgiving her, let me tell you, it was

not easy. It took several times for me to forgive her, and send her love and gratitude. The first five times I said I forgave her were absolute failures! As soon as I said the words, I thought, "Who are you kidding?" But then I began remembering stories my dad had told me about the antics he and Aunt Gin pulled as children and how she protected him. When he was sent to his room for bad behavior, Aunt Gin would sneak him snacks, crayons, and toys. As adults, Aunt Gin and her husband Uncle Henry would visit and play cards with my parents at the kitchen table. They would play for hours. Dad always looked forward to Gin's arrival. He loved her very much. I loved my dad very much. That love my dad had for his sister provided the pathway for me to begin to forgive. As I began to truly forgive Aunt Gin, a memory surfaced, a memory of a kind act on her part toward me. Her son, my cousin Ben, played guitar. He had his first guitar, which was his learning guitar. When he outgrew it, Aunt Gin brought it on her next visit and gave it to me. Maybe she had heard about the piano fiasco, I don't know. But I do know I really appreciated it. I never thought I'd have a guitar! I guess I must have been in fourth grade at the time. My mother found introductory guitar instruction books and then paid for me to take lessons at a nearby music store. I was more relaxed with a guitar. Five strings and one hand remembering notes and chords sure beat 88 keys and two hands trying to remember everything. I had a great time with that little guitar. When I mastered the introductory lessons, my parents helped me to get a better guitar. My practice guitar gift was plastic. My new guitar was wooden with steel strings. In the end, I had to face the fact I was not musically inclined. I could play some folk songs and play many chord combinations, and sing off-key, but I never developed a real talent for music. To this day, I like to fool around with the guitar and I listen to music much of the time.

I was finally able to find forgiveness for my Aunt Gin. When the forgiveness was genuine, I could feel the energy flowing and my ability to raise my vibration even higher.

Ask your Higher Self, your Spirit Guide, Spirit, or whoever you work with from the other side to help you identify areas in your life that need your attention relative to forgiveness. Forgive yourself if you want to hold on to unforgiveness, as I did for my Aunt Gin. Forgive yourself if you see areas of your life where you know you fell short. Those areas include purposely harming another person by gossip, physical, mental or emotional abuse, anger, etc. If that person is alive and would benefit from knowingly receiving your forgiveness, then forgive in person or ask to be forgiven in person. However, if it would harm the other person, then forgive in your heart. Forgiveness is a huge key to a fulfilled and prosperous life. And remember, you are clearing your energy through forgiveness, so you are the one who truly benefits from forgiveness.

CHAPTER 10
FIRST STEPS

The first steps to deliberately creating are to understand and accept that you are a spirit living in a borrowed or acquired body and understand and accept that your power and purpose is to create. You could have one or more life purposes during this incarnation. This purpose is known to your higher self and is revealed to you as you walk your intended path.

How do you recognize your intended path? You know it in a certain level of comfort or in moments of joy. You know you've hit on something when what you are doing in the moment causes you to be happy. Perhaps it is the way you find that you naturally, unselfishly love your family and your intention is to be the best parent you can become. Perhaps it is the joy you feel at work when you solve problems and cause the system to work more efficiently. Perhaps it is the happiness you feel when you get your first rushing down on the football field. You get that glimpse of your life purpose(s) when you experience that rush of joy or of happiness.

When you decide you want to manifest something into your life, you need to feel that same joy or happiness. This helps you set your intention. You can manufacture that same joy artificially, by remembering a joyful experience. Completely immerse yourself in that experience and then while feeling this joy, focus on your intention and hold it there for at least 20 seconds. By doing this, I am able to replace low-energy vibration thoughts with high-energy vibration thoughts by simply remembering how much fun Sam (my Border Collie) has when I am throwing the ball for him. Even better, if I am able to actually throw the ball for him at the moment, we both benefit. You will be able to manufacture the high-vibration emotions by remembering your joyful experiences. If you have been in love and remember the early days, when all you wanted was to connect with your loved one, and felt joy when you saw him or her—those are high-vibration feelings and they will put you into the right place for setting your intention.

You may say that you have done that but you have not experienced positive results, or even have experienced negative results. The reason is that you really do get what you believe to be true. If you are trying to manifest abundance and are visualizing yourself living a life of wealthy celebrity, your conscious mind (or your ego) knows without a doubt that you work for a limited wage and you work every day at a job you'd gladly give up if you won the lottery. Because if your ego does not believe what you are visualizing, it will not happen.

But there are techniques for successful manifesting.

First, ask yourself if what you are trying to manifest is something you are moving *toward* or are moving *away from.* For example, if you are trying to manifest a new job, is it because you are dissatisfied with your current job (you are in job hell) and are desperately trying to get away from it? If so, your attention is really fixed on your current job and your strong feelings about it. You are thus moving away from that current situation, your attention is fixed on that situation, and your emotional charge rests with that situation. However, if you are moving toward a new situation instead of away from an old one, your emotional charge will rest with the new situation.

In order to move towards instead of moving away, you need to accept your current situation. For example, you accept your current job and are grateful for it. However meager or unpleasant it may be, it is bringing you some level of income and allowing you to successfully exist. If you are reading this, I assume you are sustaining life. You need to go to work each day and do your very best in each moment. Being grateful in the moment will reduce the negative emotional charge you have attached to your current job, thereby opening the door to deliberate creation. You need to accept your current situation, be grateful, and set your intention on your heart's desire. You need to increase the positive charge with higher-vibration thoughts and emotions, and decrease the negative charge with acceptance and gratefulness. As long as you give out negative vibration emotions and thoughts or mixed emotions and thoughts, you will not manifest what you desire in your life.

Second, you must also be aware of your dominant thoughts throughout the day. Are you thinking negative thoughts about others or about yourself? Are you living in the past or the future? Are you living in your head or are you living from your heart? When you make the decision to monitor your thoughts, you will be surprised at what you catch yourself thinking and how those thoughts interfere with your ability to create the life you want. Just make a decision to monitor or observe your thoughts. You will then be able to immediately stop a negative thought and switch your thinking to a higher vibration. For example, you want to manifest a new car, but then you find yourself thinking you cannot afford that new car. Change your thoughts and raise your vibration immediately. Another example: you want to manifest a new job and you find yourself thinking how much you hate the job you are currently doing. Again, you can change your thoughts and raise your vibration just by finding something to appreciate right in that moment. It may be thoughts of your life partner or an area in your life that is going well. It may be something as small as being thankful you have money to buy groceries this week.

Third, your first deliberate creation should be something believable for you. Your ego will not accept that you currently live in a four-bedroom, three-bathroom home overlooking the ocean if you live in a two-bedroom apartment overlooking the city. Also, do *not* pick manifesting a great parking space. Great parking spaces are nice, but getting one could be just luck. You need to manifest a desire that will not be confused with luck.

Yes, surely, "luck" could really be the result of your intention (I habitually manifest great parking spaces) but for this exercise, please select something specific that will cause you to smile when it comes into your life.

Fourth, manifest a desire that does not lock in *how* it will be accomplished.

Fifth, you need to be detached from the outcome. You should not try to manifest something you need right now. Until you are comfortable with the process, you shouldn't try to manifest money for next week's rent because you will be worrying about that on some level and by worrying and being tied into the outcome, the process of deliberate creation will be blocked. Your first successful deliberate creation should be something that holds either no negative emotional charge or very little emotional charge. More on that later.

CHAPTER 11
IF YOU ALWAYS DO WHAT YOU'VE ALWAYS DONE YOU'LL ALWAYS GET WHAT YOU ALWAYS GOT

Reading the same information over and over does not cause growth or change. Doing the same things over and over does not cause growth or change. Thinking the same thoughts over and over does not cause growth or change. Why do we expect a different outcome by using the same methods that we always use? If we continue to use the same methods, we will continue to garner the same results.

In order for the results in your life to change, you have to change the way you go about bringing results into your life, and do it while operating under the laws of the universe. This is easier said than done.

You must begin by placing your trust in the universe and not in your ego. In other words, you must let go of what you perceive as control and accept whatever happens in your life. You will be told different methods in later chapters but for now, you need to understand that in order to create anything deliberately and without stress, you will need to let go of control and place 100% of your faith in the universe or source energy. I use the word universe but it is interchangeable with source energy or God. You may have other names.

Also, the law of allowing is detaching yourself from the outcome. That is why your first deliberate creation must be focused on something specific but without an emotional charge attached. Your first deliberate creation cannot be something you really need. Instead, it must be something readily accepted by your ego as being possible and cannot be attached to an emotionally charged outcome. The law of allowing is the step where most people fail. They fail to detach themselves emotionally from what they are trying to create. So begin thinking about what you'd like to create that is totally believable to your ego. It could be a bookcase, new jeans, car tires—anything that is specific and believable.

CHAPTER 12
CREATIVE VS. COMPETITIVE

We arrived on this plane with the ability to create. We are creating all the time. In addition to creating on purpose, we need to understand that creation and competition are not compatible. Now, I like competition when it comes to things like sports. In fact, I am a dyed-in-the-wool Patriots football fan. I have been their fan since the days when they could not get out of their own way and winning a game was an unusual occurrence. I enjoy competition in areas such as sports, movies and music awards, etc.

However, the deliberate creator does not need to engage in competition that harms others. The deliberate creator knows there is enough "stuff" for everyone. The deliberate creator knows that becoming wealthy does not mean someone else has to be poor. The deliberate creator knows that abundance is infinite and does not need to steal, cheat, or stoop to low means of gaining wealth. The deliberate creator will offer a hand to someone who needs it. The deliberate creator will not, under any circumstances, enter into business deals that will lessen, diminish, hurt, or cheat others. Stepping on others to get ahead is a result of living in your head and believing in limitation. We should, rather, live in this world, knowing we help ourselves to become wealthy to enjoy all the good things life has to offer and also help others enjoy these wonderful things. If we need to cheat to win or if we need to step on someone else to get ahead, then we are not even close to the freedom and generosity available to deliberate creators.

When we create we are not competing. There is no stress, hostility, anger, or fear associated with deliberate creation. Deliberate creation is easy, loving, light, and grateful.

What do you do, if you are in a profession that requires you to cheat, harm or lessen others? First, accept it and be thankful for where you are right now. Then give your intention over to the desire to get to a position where you can deliberately create a life that is easy, loving, grateful, and abundant.

CHAPTER 13
TIME AND FREE WILL

When we came to this life, we came with limitations. As spirit beings between lives, we are able to instantly manifest our desires. When we come to this life, we come with the burden—and the gift—of time.

Time is actually an illusion. The only time we can act is right now. Our power is right now. We cannot change the past or act in the future. We can only act right now. Our power is right now. When we are using our ego or our consciousness to make our decisions, we are making our decisions based on past experience. Yes, we try new things, but we rely on our old decision making processes. Our ego only knows what is stored in our past. The pain we have experienced, both physically and emotionally, are experiences our ego tries to protect us from experiencing again. Our ego tries to prevent us from experiencing life in the present moment because the ego has no frame of reference for living in the present moment. Most of us find ourselves living in the past or in the future. Very few of us live in the present moment without thought of the past or the future.

When we commit a negative act, we do not feel the impact of that act right away. But what goes around does come around. You do reap what you sow. However, there is the bumper of time. You may have harmed others by spreading lies and rumors about them, but you may not feel the consequence until much later. The consequence may turn up in a financial downturn, failing health, or in your own reputation being destroyed. But, no matter what, if you send negativity into the universe it will return to you multiplied.

If, however, we felt the impact of an action immediately following either our loving intention or our destructive act, we would behave more like trained animals who do tricks for treats. If we were punished immediately for promoting the destruction of someone else, we would not engage in negative activity. However, we would make our choice to love out of fear of punishment instead of out of the desire to love and make this world a better place. In other words, if there were no such thing as the buffer of time, we would really not have the freedom to exercise free will.

If you realize that you are responsible for destructive thoughts and acts, you can do one of two things. You can wait for your negativity to come back to you multiplied or you can begin making repairs. Only you know what you have done, so you must be very honest with yourself and decide which road you will take. If you decide to make repairs, please do not make matters worse in doing so. Own up to your mistakes, ask forgiveness, forgive yourself, and move forward with love. Do not keep thinking about the past. Make repairs, ask forgiveness, forgive yourself and move on. If those persons have already passed, you can still ask for forgiveness. Remember then, forgive yourself and move forward with love.

Time is our friend and our challenge. Time allows us to experience free will because there is no instant manifestation. But it can frustrate us, for the same reason.

So you must remember to live in the moment; your point of power is *now*. Your power is not in yesterday's thoughts or tomorrow's worries. Your power is now. When you put your intention out to the universe, it is now. When your intention is manifested, it is manifested now. You have power in this moment.

The author Eric Tolle provides excellent information relative to living in the present moment.

CHAPTER 14
KNOW WHAT YOU DON'T WANT

This sounds too simple, but the first step to deliberate creation is to know what you don't want. You need to be specific and you need to be brief.

You are probably a master of getting what you don't want, so no doubt you know what you don't want. In fact, you think about what you don't want way too often. You may think that you do not want to be poor. You may often worry about how the bills will be paid, or if you will have the rent money this month or the food money this week. You may worry about the horrendous price of gas, knowing you have to put gas in the tank to get to work to make the meager amount of money to pay the rent. But your fixed income stays fixed (your weekly pay), while the price of gas goes up. This is real and painful daily existence. Yet as you worry about the lack of money, you innocently attract more lack of money into your life.

So if you want to attract more money into your

life, you have to change your everyday thinking and police your dominant thoughts. When you observe yourself worrying about having enough money to pay the bills, immediately switch your thoughts from worry to being grateful about something—anything! Doing this will raise your vibration and, little by little, your situation will change for the better.

Decide what you don't want. Do not dwell on what you don't want. Just make a decision about one item and then leave it.

CHAPTER 15
DECIDE WHAT YOU DO WANT

Decide what you want but do not use the word *want* in your intention statement. Never use any word that implies lack. For example, if you say you want more money, you imply you do not have enough money and you are sending the message of lack into the universe. The universe will respond to your message of lack with more of the same.

The word *desire* implies positive anticipation. For example, if you say you desire to increase your income, you are sending a positive message of desire and the universe will respond positively to your desire. The word desire does not imply you are lacking, only that you are joyously looking forward.

When you decide what you want, be specific. Do not focus on more than one intention. If your desire is financial abundance, do not use the word *abundance*. What does abundance mean to the universe? You must be specific and you must be reality-based. I mentioned earlier that your ego or your conscious self has to believe what you are saying. If your intention is a picture of you living in a four-bedroom, three-bathroom home overlooking the ocean with a BMW in the private driveway, your conscious self will never believe you. As a result, you will give mixed messages to the universe and your intention will not be manifested.

Instead of tackling the house on the beach right now, set your intention for a more realistic goal. For example, if you are earning $20,000 a year right now, you could set your intention to attract $30,000 within the coming twelve months. You need to open the door to your ego to allow the $30,000 intention to reach your subconscious in order for you to attract that additional $10,000. You do this by telling the universe that you "intend to attract $30,000 into your life within the coming twelve months." Be very specific about the amount of money you wish to attract and be very specific to use the phrase that you INTEND to attract that amount of money into your life within the coming twelve months. Your conscious self knows you do not make $30,000 a year but it will accept the fact that you intend to attract that amount of money. Once your conscious self or your ego accepts your intention as fact, the subconscious will then begin the process of attracting it into your life.

If your desire is to be a smaller dress size, the same approach applies. And before you even start, you have been looking into your eyes a minimum of every morning and every evening and telling yourself that you love yourself fully and unconditionally. Having said this, your step to creating a healthier body is the same as for creating additional income.

State your desire in positive terms. For example: "I intend to lose fifteen pounds in the next eight weeks. My intention is that my body is healthy and is perfect in weight and size."

Don't forget. Set your intention with emotions that sustain high vibrations, like the feelings you had when you first fell in love.

CHAPTER 16
ACTION

You have just read that you need to decide what you want and, after making that decision, you set your intention with positive words and feelings.

Setting your believable intention with positive words and strong, high-vibration feelings allows the subconscious to begin to attract from the universe to you the desires you have expressed.

There is no cookie-cutter recipe for when to add action into your intention, but at some time action will be required. It is very unlikely you will hit the lottery and be instantly wealthy. Instead, your intentions will be attracted to you by the work of your subconscious and the response of the universe by the law of attraction.

If your intention is to attract an additional $10,000 into your life within the coming twelve months, then look for the opportunities to reveal themselves: new ways to earn additional income, job promotions, opportunities to reduce expenses, etc. You will have to apply for that new work position or overtime opportunity. Yes, you set your intention with high vibrations following the advice you have read so far, and you expect to see or experience your intention becoming manifest. But if you set your intention to lose fifteen pounds in the coming three months, you must also act. You must consider calories, exercise, and overall health. You selected your body and you know what your body needs. You may have always failed in the past when trying to lose weight, but you were working from your head instead of your heart and spirit. In the past you worked from a low vibration of guilt, embarrassment, and the like, but now you are setting an intention from a high vibration of love and acceptance. You will see that if you bring your vibration up to a higher level several times a day while holding this intention, you will see results.

CHAPTER 17
CLEAR YOUR ENERGY
TO RECEIVE

N ow, let's go back to your energy centers, known as chakras. I had learned that energy should flow upward through the chakra system and it should flow freely and be maintained over the course of time. I also learned that if an energy center is blocked, your energy does not move freely and the energy blockage impacts your ability to raise your vibration. I decided that if it is important for my energy to flow freely, I needed to learn how to make it happen.

Because my knowledge about the chakra system and how to work with it could fit in a thimble, I decided to put the intention out to the universe to attract to me the person or persons who would help me in this area.

Within twenty-four hours, the universe began to respond to my request. I heard people talking about energy work and I saw information about it in magazines. To make a long story short, I found a

63

woman named Marlene Campbell. She is a Licensed Massage Therapist, Registered Polarity Practitioner, RYSE Practitioner, and Quantum Touch instructor. She completed training in Shamanic Practice, Lightwork, and Earth Stewardship. She also practiced in the New England area, so I knew I hit the jackpot! Her website is www.rippleeffectworkshops.com. If you are ready to work with your energy centers, I recommend Marlene without reservation. She offers sessions in person and by telephone consultation for individuals and animals. In addition, she conducts workshops in New England and other areas, by request.

I attended a Quantum Touch workshop led by Marlene. At that workshop, I found deeper levels of unforgiveness in me that I was holding on to, and I was able to release them. I began to understand my energy centers and was taught how to keep the energy flowing by focusing and high vibration. I had also broken two toes on my right foot. I hobbled into her home and by the middle of the second day, my toes were healed. This workshop deepened my understanding of the importance of energy and how we are all one.

Because I have no expertise and very little experience working with energy, I recommend that you address your energy flow by contacting a person who works with energy, someone with similar credentials to Marlene's.

CHAPTER 18
RAISE YOUR VIBRATION

I suggested ways to emotionally raise your vibration in Chapter Four. I want to take time now to describe another powerful way of raising energy. This is through deliberate breathing and sweeping.

I learned to do this at the Quantum Touch workshop taught by Marlene Campbell. Quantum Touch is an effective tool for those who practice hands-on healing. Unlike some disciplines, like Reiki, there are no attunements or levels involved. It utilizes focus, breathing, hand positions, and touch. The main lesson I took away from the workshop weekend was how to raise my vibration even higher.

Sweeping is a technique to put you in touch with your energy, running from your feet to your head, back down through your shoulders and down through your arms, and out of your hands. The basic idea is that energy follows thought and that wherever you place your attention, the energy follows.

We began to learn to sweep by first holding one

finger in the air for a minute or two. During that time, we tuned into our finger by focusing on intensifying our awareness of the finger. We were told to feel how the skin wrapped around the finger, etc. Marlene instructed us to feel our finger completely. Some of us felt very little sensation and others felt tingling. The point was to feel our life force and recognize that where we focus our attention is where the energy will follow.

We selected a partner and each person would have a turn running energy on his or her partner. Simply put, the exercise had each of us moving our hands up the partner's body from feet to head. Our hands were either not touching or lightly touching the other person. Some people could feel warmth from the other's hands, but no healing was taking place at that time; it was practice to begin sensing the life force energy within each of us.

Lightly stroke yourself from your toes to your knees and stop. Feel any sensations. Repeat the stroke and feel the sensations. Now continue to lightly stoke yourself, working your strokes up to your head then back down your shoulders and out to your hands. Do this one arm at a time.

Now with your imagination, see yourself receiving a full body sweep but without moving your hands over your body. Sense the energy moving up from your feet to your head and down through your arms and out of your hands. Do these sweeps quickly. Energy moves quickly. So don't apply a lot of concentration, which will slow things down. Just go through the movements quickly in your imagination, feeling the energy moving up through your body to your head and then quickly down though your shoulders and out from your hands.

The next step is to learn a breathing technique that you will use with the sweeping exercise you just did.

Breathing techniques are central to running energy. If you are a shallow breather, or an upper chest breather, this exercise may seem foreign to you. Most people tend to be shallow breathers from the stomach area or upper chest breathers. I am an upper chest breather, and I remain an upper chest breather unless I focus on raising my vibration! Every one of the techniques I learned requires full breaths that push the belly out when you inhale. You breathe in through your nose and exhale through your nose unless you are breathing so deeply that you must use your mouth to feel comfortable. It doesn't matter if you use your nose or your mouth to inhale or exhale, because the techniques work equally well. Take a full breath now and cup your hands under your belly button. Feel your belly expand with your inhalation. Breathe so deeply that your shoulders move up just a little.

We were taught several breathing techniques. My favorite is, for me, the easiest. It is called the 4-4 breath. Count to four as you inhale and do a full body sweep allowing the energy to reach your head (this should be done quickly). Then as you exhale, allow all the sensation to run from your shoulders into your hands. All the while, feel all sensations as fully as possible. Continue to practice sweeping and breathing until you begin to feel your vibration rising. At that time, begin to imagine whatever it is that makes you smile—whatever makes your heart full. It could be the exhilaration of skiing down a mountain on packed powder, sun shining. It could be watching your child learn to walk. It could be a baby smiling for the first time. It could be the day you were married. Bring to mind whatever it is that brings you joy and happiness. You should now be breathing, running energy, and smiling because you are picturing your joy. Remember to continue to breathe because the energy will stop flowing if you hold your breath. While holding your high vibration in this state of joy, turn your attention to your intention and give it to the universe. Continue to breathe, sweep, and be full of joy for fifteen seconds. Do this several times a day, if possible, when you desire to manifest something into your life.

I remember thinking that this exercise of sweeping, breathing, and imagining joy felt foolish, but I quickly told myself that if it works, it's fine with me!

Even if you have no interest in energy healing, Quantum Touch will help you learn to increase your vibration to new and wonderful heights. The foundation of Quantum Touch is love and gratitude.

I recommend that you read the book *Quantum Touch: The Power to Heal*, by Richard Gordon and that you take a Quantum Touch basic class if you can. Again, take a look at www.rippleeffectworkshops.com to get a better idea of what I am trying to say here.

CHAPTER 19
THE MAGIC BOX

Several authors I have read mentioned using boxes for the purpose of manifesting. Some have suggested we cut out pictures of our desires and place them in the box, or write notes about them. Some have suggested we lavishly decorate the box. I have heard these boxes described as prayer boxes, where letters to God are placed. Although I found the reading enjoyable, none of this resonated with me. However, Dr. Robert Anthony described the use of his box as, well, almost as a mailbox. The full description of this is in his audio book *The Secret of Deliberate Creation.*

The "magic box" answered the questions I had about the law of allowing. As you know, the law of allowing is the most difficult step in manifesting your desires. In order to allow your intention to manifest, you must let go of it and divorce yourself from the outcome. It's just like when you go to a restaurant for dinner. The waiter or waitress, after taking your order, disappears from your sight, perhaps into the kitchen or the bar to deliver your order for the specific meal you requested. You don't then jump up to follow your server to make sure he or she is using the correct ingredients for your drink or appetizer. You don't run back to the kitchen to check food labels or to ask the chef for his or her credentials. What do you do? You remain seated at your table, talk with your companion, and maybe take a sip of water. You expect warm bread rolls, and perhaps your appetizer and drink, to flawlessly arrive. What I am saying here is that you do not concern yourself with all the *hows* of your meal order. You believe your server gathered the correct information and delivered it to the correct people, who would prepare and deliver your meal to your table. How they handled all the details in the creation of your dining experience was known only to them. You enjoyed the outcome. That is the secret of allowing. So, how do you discipline yourself not to jump up and follow your waiter or waitress into the kitchen? The answer for me was to use a magic box.

I realized that I needed a way to effectively *allow* without concerning myself with the *how*. I bought a 6" x 4" box from a large discount store. It is bright blue metal and cost $4.99. I instructed my circle of family (from Chapter Two, where I described my visit to my life between lives), as well as my higher self and my helping and guiding angels, that whenever I placed an intention in that box, I was giving it over to them. It was like giving my meal order over to the wait staff at the restaurant.

The first intention I placed in my box was so specific that I actually included the *how*. I said that not only did I want a better job, but I wanted a job that was currently available. I had a negative experience because I did not get that particular job. When I discovered additional information about that particular job, I was relieved I did not get it because it would have been going from the frying pan into the fire, so to speak. The universe really does know more than we know!

So I then placed the intention into my magic box that I would manifest an additional $5,000 or better during the next three months and that I would enjoy the process. Almost immediately, I received three offers to teach at a local community college—to the tune of $6000. I enjoy teaching and I was thankful and happy!

Another example: my house needed a new roof. I alerted my squad (my circle of family, highest self, angels, etc) that I intended to manifest a new metal roof and keep the cost around $3500. Roofers gave me estimates between $4500–$6000. But, instead of trying to figure out the *hows*, I left my faith in my magic mailbox. I knew my intention was given to the universe, just as my meal order is given to my wait staff. A few weeks later, an old acquaintance reappeared in my life. He had done some excavation work for me in the past and had replaced my old furnace with a new, energy-efficient one. He said he noticed that I could use a new roof and that his company could do the job for me if I wanted. He dropped off a color chart of metal roofing for me to look at, measured the roof, and calculated the expense. If I could wait until October, his company could do the job for $3500.

Those are two examples of allowing my intention to manifest without meddling in how the intentions were to be accomplished. The little blue metal box has been magic for me. This is how I place my order.

- I write my intention down.
- I verbally alert *my circle of family, my higher self, my helping angels, and the universe* (don't want to leave anyone out).
- I read my intention out loud (reading it out loud is not necessary, but I like doing it this way).
- I ask that my intention, or something better, be manifested.
- I give thanks and gratitude.
- I place it in the box.

Once I place it in the box, I leave it there. I'll be sure to be thankful each day and to visualize the outcome many times during the day. You will see that when you change your thoughts to focus on the outcome instead of the process, you begin to see changes in the world around you and you begin to see your intention manifest in this world. This could be in relationships, career, health, and so on. This box will help you totally let go of the process that involve the *hows*. Hows are left up to the universe to decide. You simply place your order and anticipate miracles with an attitude of gratitude and love.

CHAPTER 20
BACK TO ALICE

In order to manifest your best and highest good, you must simply understand Wonderland. Alice learned to obey the laws of Wonderland by dealing with the various characters along the way. In the book, Alice sees a white rabbit, dressed in a coat, run by, muttering that he will be late. She follows the rabbit down the rabbit hole and finds herself falling into a different world, where she has several adventures. She meets and learns lessons from the Cheshire Cat, the Mad Hatter, the March Hare, and the unforgettable Queen of Hearts.

Down the Rabbit Hole is a term for going on an adventure into the unknown. There are other meanings attached to this term, but they are not germane to this little book.

Each of us decided to go down the rabbit hole when we came to this life from the other side. We encounter many different people and characters in our lifetime and each of them, friend or foe, can teach us valuable lessons. We learn to navigate in this physical dimension, much like Alice did. But like Alice, we must challenge the Queen of Hearts and find our way back to the reality we left behind.

That means we must live from our higher self and bring love to this world. We are here to create for ourselves and for others. When we make the decision to love, we experience miracles. If you want to see miracles happen in your life, then help someone else to be successful. Help someone else to attain what you would like to attain. That is love in action: to want the same or better for others. When you put that intention and action out to the world, the universe will reward you in bigger and better ways than you could ever imagine.

If you read this little book and practice its lessons, and find you still need help to attain your first deliberate creation, please email me at: **kmackenzie123@gmail.com**. I'll be happy to help you manifest your first deliberate creation.